Copyright © October 4, 2015 by Chenae' L. Hammond. All rights reserved. Published in the United States of America.
Second edition.

No part of this book may be reproduced or transmitted in any form, or by any means, electronic or mechanical, including photocopying, recording or by any information storage or retrieval system without written permission from the publisher.

I Almost Held On
Church Girl Inc.
ISBN: 0692591311

Layout and Design: J'Marie Design Studios
Photography: Elizabeth Ashley & Co.

Volume I: *Vent: The Different Faces Of Me*
Church Girl Inc.
Durham, North Carolina
Churchgirlinc.com

Welcome Back

Introduction

In my last book, I talked a lot about what writing does for me on the inside. Poetry has been therapeutic for me for over 15 years now. When I first began writing, the thought of my poetry turning into books had not crossed my mind.

This book will be similar but it differs from *Vent: The Different Faces Of Me*. This book is broken into three parts but this project will probably hit you at your core so I had to break this book up and go deep. I had some experiences over the past couple years that hit me at my core so I figured I would write about it. After all, like I said in my first book, poetry is therapy for me as I hope it is for you.

Sometimes **God has to make you hit rock bottom so He can show you that He is the rock at the bottom**. He will put you in a place where you will not have anyone else to depend on but Him because God is the only one who can actually bring you through it. You can have all the conversations in the world with family, friends, pastors, or whomever you seek advice from. But God is truly the only one who can help you endure and make it to the end of your process. You just have to trust Him.

We have all heard the saying, "The truth shall set you free." I was on social media one day and I happened to be scrolling through a bishop's instagram page. One of the things I read was, "God cannot deliver you from the things you will not confront." Those of us who are churchgoers will admit that the minute we hear something good we want to fall on the floor (lol). That statement alone hit me in a place where I had to realize that no matter what was happening to me at the time, I had to confront what I never wanted to face. I wanted God to truly heal and deliver me from the things that tormented me. I didn't realize how hurt I was until God humbled me and took me through a very dreadful yet fulfilling process that broke me until there was nothing else to break. I had many sleepless nights, I was in a frantic state all the time, and no one could talk sense into me. I completely thought I was losing my mind.

It was in those frantic and fearful moments where I really experienced the power of God. Many of us declare to love God and have a special place in our hearts for Him. However, sometimes that statement is contingent on the blessings opposed to the suffering. I had the learn the true meaning of depending on God, focusing on God, and trusting in Him when I didn't know what He was doing in me. God tested me and consistently asked me, "Would you serve me if I never gave you what you asked for? Am I only good for you when **you think** I'm being good to you? Are you a **willing** warrior or a weak warrior? Will you **fight** or will you **fold**?" I had to answer these questions before I realized that if I was going to serve God, I had to serve God through anything.

One thing I will say about my process (or my journey) is that I am not only a survivor, but I have the ability to thrive. For a long time, I thought something was wrong with me. I couldn't keep friends and everyone seemed to be there temporarily. In one of my poems, I use a phrase that says, "Chenae, you would rather carry around dead people than be without people…" My friend, Melissa (*Mel*), told me that and I have carried that with me ever since. Mostly (not all) relationships I have had with people have been handpicked by me without God's approval. I was so afraid of losing people and letting go that I was carrying around dead people and dead weight that was only draining me. I didn't realize that I was comfortable in dead relationships. Mel said to me, "Being comfortable doesn't mean you are in bliss because you can be comfortably tormented and be comfortable in that." I sat back and said to her, "YOU DON'T KNOW MY LIFE!" You know we get defensive when the people who love us are right (lol).

I got to a point where I wanted to come out of the torment because I wanted to live that abundant life that the bible speaks about. In order for me to do that, I knew I had to endure and let go. That was a hard thing for me because I never really knew how to let go and not feel bad. I knew what it felt like to be let go of. I also knew what it felt like to be given up on. Since I knew the feeling, I never wanted anyone to feel that pain. Well, God gave me an assignment to let go and I took heed. God had to rid me of every insecurity and the chains that were keeping me from being free.

My biggest downfall has been people but my greatest accomplishment came from my courageous spirit to walk away. Even in being misunderstood and growing pains, God promised me that He was going to make my life better if I agreed to follow Him. He further taught me that agreeing to follow Him comes with believing Him, listening to Him, and loving Him. If you trust God, He will carry you through your darkest days.

Everything you get into is a process. Every negative belief you have about yourself didn't happen overnight. So whatever process you are in, trust that God is going to bring you through. If you lose people along the way, that just means that God is stripping you of the dirt so the diamond in you can shine. I hope you are encouraged after reading this because God has great things in store for you. Trust the process. I still have to tell myself that.

I wrote this book because I wanted to let people know that you have the ability to be free from anything. The process may hurt but the promise is worth it. This book will be for the people who are misunderstood. It will be for the people who feel like they have been abandoned, afraid, alone, or apprehensive to talk about things they have bottled up inside. It is for those who wish they could achieve their victory overnight but who are **willing to endure** the process that has been set before them. It is for the people who have had suicidal thoughts, spiritual warfare, fear, loneliness, anxiety, and other painful symptoms where the physical pain is easier to bear than the pain on the inside. It is for the people who don't know how to fight this fight in the natural, so they have no choice but to fight in the spiritual realm. It is for those who don't know how to speak up. This book is here to help you and me.

As you read this, I pray it blesses you just as much as I was blessed when I was given the assignment to write it. Take this journey of healing, deliverance, and freedom with me and LET'S DIG DEEP!

Table of Contents

"Watch What You Say: The 'I Can't' Syndrome"
Dating Success
Confirmation
What Makes You Beautiful
At The Altar
Getting Closer
The Fight
A State Of Maturity
Strength
Used

"Let It Go"
My Season #1
At The Forefront
Freedom
Galatians 1:10
I Am Willing
Elephant
Blessed
I'm A Follower

"Moving Forward"
I'm Next
Here I am
The Wedding
I Am Eve
Amazing

Opportunity
Even Jesus
A Letter To Jesus

This book is dedicated to every person who has helped me and is still helping me overcome. I love you. Thank you.

"Don't hold on to the things that God is trying to break you away from. The more you hold on, the less freedom you will have. Your words are part of your deliverance. Use them."
~Chenae'

"Watch What You Say: The 'I Can't Syndrome'"

"The power of life and death are in the tongue and those who love it will eat its fruit." -Proverbs 18:21 (NIV)

Words are very powerful. I am only in my 20s so God willing I have a long life to live. In the 20 years that I have been on this earth, I have often caught myself saying things like, "I can't." I didn't realize that starting a sentence with 'I can't' would completely affect the rest of my thoughts or the way I would go about things. When anyone would ask me if I would be able to get pass a certain situation, I would say, "I can't." At some point, I had to dig deep down inside myself and figure out why I thought I couldn't do something. I found that the reason why I said "I can't" was because I was scared. I was actually scared of being victorious. I know that sounds weird. You're probably thinking to yourself, "How can she be scared to be victorious or have some type of victory?" It's very easy to do because it's a mindset. As a Christian, I have learned that the devil plays with your mind so much that you will begin to believe you can't or won't be able to do something or overcome something. He plays with your mind so much that he will completely make you believe something that is contradictory to what is in your heart. You have to be careful because he can literally put you in a hostage situation. But you have to remember, the devil is a liar!

This part of the book will be focused on choosing your words wisely. When I was in law school, I remember talking to my professor, Nakia C. Davis (PD), and I remember telling her that I was depressed. She told me that I said the word "depressed" about 5-7 times in the first 30 seconds of our conversation. She told me, "Hammond, watch your words because they are powerful. I want you to hold on to something. You are only living what you will talk about later." Before that conversation, I didn't realize how many times I spoke death over myself. I was so used to saying "I can't" or "I'm sad." Every time I said it, I felt it more and more throughout the day. The bible says in 1 Peter 3:10, "For whomever would love life and see good days must keep their tongue from evil and their lips from deceitful speech." Speak positively even if you don't feel it. The more you give yourself words of affirmation, the better you will feel.

There were times when things didn't go my way and I thought I failed. I would call home and tell my mom and aunt that I was ready to move back home because I felt like I was failing. Many people had walked out of my life and at the time, I didn't know that God was demanding me to release some people. Every time I got weary or had a bad day, I would always hear my mom's voice say, "Chenae, you haven't failed at anything. You actually have more courage than anyone I know. **I want you to remember something, we don't fail, we fix it**." The funny thing is I'm shedding tears while writing this because I didn't realize how powerful that statement was until I genuinely had to apply it.

Watch what you say because what you say will change your life, including the way you think, what affects you, and the confidence you have about your situation. Don't hold on to your 'I can't syndrome.' Lay it down and walk away from it.

Dating Success

I made a date with success
After being tossed and turned by life
And wrapped by a knife
That stabbed my life
Until I bled tears of wanting success
I made a date with success
Because it saw my eyes
As they cried
Cried as hard as they could
But instead of crying what cleanses you
I cried wood
Hard and dry
I cried until my eyes puffed
Until I looked in the mirror and I couldn't recognize myself
After giving a man
And friends
And family
My riches and wealth
My eyes made it so that my body couldn't recognize itself
So every time I walked I wanted to run
When I ran I wanted to scream
When I screamed I wanted to fall asleep
But when I slept I wanted to dream
Of being successful
So I made my date with success
Realizing that I had to go through some things to get there
I had to fall in love and lose myself

Get slapped by people who bruised my self
Get kicked out of school to use myself
So God could isolate me and choose myself
I had to be without a job
Sleep sleepless nights
To wake up in fear
And convince myself that everything would be all right
I had to break down a few times
As time refused to rewind itself
So I could do things differently
Forgetting that time waits for no one
And every second
Of every minute
Of every hour
Time left me wondering whether I was going to pick my face up and walk
Or was I going to put my faith on a timer
And only use it during happy times
Then lay it down by the riverside since the only time I took time to exercise my faith was when it had timed out
I have no doubt that I am a warrior in love with success
This mess that confined me will turn into something blessed
I realized that what is left to come is my best
So since one day I will marry Canaan
I have no problem with dating my wilderness
Because dates don't waste time that you spent
They only prepare you for the main event
They caution the wind to think twice

And before it rains
His Canaan is an umbrella on my life
It protects me from the storm
While it is erupting
It keeps me dry
While I'm still trusting
I've dated success even when it didn't feel like it
Even when the devil put a wall through it
And I decided that I would get to Canaan
Even if I had to crawl to it
So I got on my knees
And rhymed
To God I wasn't a waste of time
I went from being happy to being anxious
But I decided that my faith was what I was going to keep
Even when I was homeless
And didn't have a place to sleep
I got on my knees anyway
And decided to lift my hands
I decided to hide in worship
Even when I didn't understand
I found myself on the other side
After being isolated and confused
Not realizing that my wilderness was what He used
He told me that patience comes in three forms
To trust, to believe, and to keep moving forward
Even when I felt scorned
Dating is only temporary

But you have to endure it even when it's raining
Because once you decide to date your wilderness
You will say "I do" to Canaan

Confirmation

"Proof which shows that something is true or correct"
Now let's reflect on what I'm referring to
They said I could do it
They said I would be successful
But did they say it because they meant it
Or did they say it because they liked to hear themselves talk
I wonder if they know about the long nights
The long hours
The long minutes it takes to succeed on the path I chose
"Proof which shows that something is true or correct"
I'm living my dream
The very thing I've always wanted to do
It may take hard work
But I owe it all to you
All the sleepless nights I will overcome
All the times my faith got a hit
I had a voice whispering inside of me
Saying "don't quit"
Hard work will pay off
Especially because this path is my deck
Each challenge is my confirmation
My proof
Which is showing
My path
True and correct

What Makes You Beautiful

I am beautiful

Beauty is in the eyes of the beholder

To behold the very things that makes me beautiful

He sees what I don't see

He pushes me to my victory

My delivery comes from my heart

The very thing that makes me beautiful

The thing that sets me apart

The thing that's truthful

I'm hopeful that even when my eyes cry

They are oiling my skin

Because just like flowers in the spring time

I will blossom in the end

I am a friend

For those who need one

I try to send encouragement

Just like the Father and His Son

The bible says to do unto others as you would have them do unto you

That's not a hard word to follow

My beauty mirrors that unlike others

I get the memo

Your smile, your voice, is beautiful

Even when cancer or alopecia causes you to lose your hair

Your are still the "baddest" thing walking

Don't let anyone take your smile away

Even those who purposefully try to do it

Because in the end
God will win
He will see you through it
Say it with me
"I am beautiful
Because I can see
I've worked hard to get to where I am
Flaws and all
I am me"

At the Altar

I'm at the altar
Front and center
Faced forward
Pressed toward the mark
I started off running here
Then I walked
Then I crawled
Not giving up on myself
All I had to do was believe that I could overcome
That I won
The battle I was in for so long
I don't have to mentally fight
God does it for me
I don't have to worry
I gave it to Him already
And when I get scared
When I was being trampled by my enemies
God protected me at the altar
I saw a vision
I was standing in the sanctuary
By myself
Broken and wanting to be healed
I went to the altar and the more I stood there
The more I was attacked
I was being spiritually slapped
And trapped by what I had been held captive to for so long
But the more I got slapped

The higher I raised my arms
The more I turned platinum
Every slap just made me stronger
Every bruise that attempted to be implanted on me healed itself
The enemy got mad and every time I came to the altar
God protected me even more
He showed me visions of my future
If I just held on
He showed me saving others
If I just held on
One more day
If I just held on tight
He showed me that the truth makes the devil upset
He showed me that I wouldn't be here forever
He showed me that I have the ability to get going even if the ones I love gives up on me
So I'm standing at the altar
It's just me and God
And even though the enemy has waited for me to get here
Even though he attacks as soon as I get there
I raise my hands higher
And higher
And higher
And I fight
And fight
Every day until I can breathe again
People have left me
Turned their backs

And gone on with their lives
But the best part in all this is I learned how to pray
I was left alone to be fearless and free
I learned how to deal and not depend on others
I learned the difference between giving up and staying on the battlefield
I learned the difference between obligation and true love
I learned the difference between torment and peace
And ultimately
I learned how to trust God

Getting Closer

Lately
I've been a little concerned
With being great
Not scared
Or frightened
Or worried
Just a little concerned
My life is changing
My heart is racing
But not in a bad way
It's like each day
I'm getting closer
And my heart is getting softer
But yet
I'm not scared
I've depended on the Most High
So I look to the sky for help
Realizing that He's the only one who can help me with myself
I'm blessed
Absolutely
So my heart is not worried
Just concerned
But in the best way
I want to handle my future with care
I want to give it all I have
I want to smile everyday knowing that I'm pleasing God
My life is changing

And that's ok

Because God is showing me that my past is just that

Every day I get closer

And every day brings on a new challenge

But I'm ready

Because I may be concerned

Any normal person would be

But I'm far from afraid

The Fight

The Lord blessed me today

I woke up this morning and got started on my way

Who am I to say that I should not go through a storm

I should only depend on God to keep me warm

He is my sunshine

My happiness

My laughter

My joy

He is something to me that not even the devil can destroy

The Lord blessed me today

He kissed my face

I opened my eyes

And was able to look at my space

I got another chance to get it right

To get myself together

To pray and walk

Even through the stormiest weather

Victory is claimed everyday

Even if I don't feel it

Although I am not fully healed

God already revealed it

So when I woke up this morning

I got another chance to get it right

To live past my darkness

To get to the light

I will get rest

I will sleep

Because my day is coming
When I will know how to reap
The Lord blessed me today
He allowed me to see
That even in the smallest moments in the day
I truly already have victory

A State Of Maturity

There are times where we can choose to quit

Not wanting to work as hard

But you will never get to your destiny

If you throw in your card

If we choose to give up

Choose to say "I quit"

How are you growing

Maturing your spirit

You have to get your sister

Take her by the hand

Tell her she can get through it

She must believe that she can

Speak life into your situation

Time will tell

Look at how God delivered you before

What He does, He does well

Quitting is not an option

Just endure

Because in due time God will bring you through

He will restore

He will keep you in perfect peace

It is never too late

Believe in the Word

Dwell in Romans 8:28

Joshua, Job, Isaiah, and Proverbs

The Word shows us

That God is sovereign

Stay close to God
He will give you more
He shows us just how good He is
In James 1: 1-4
Count it all joy when you fall into trials
Your testing produces patience through anything
But let patience have its perfect work
That you may be perfect and complete
Lacking nothing

Strength

I opened my eyes this morning
But something held me down
And down I felt
And bound
So I attempted to break free
Hoping to remain strong
I broke free
I closed my eyes and opened them again
Realizing that I was dreaming
I woke up
Waiting for my mind to focus
I waited
Wishing that I knew where my strength was
I searched and searched
And all along
I was searching the wrong place
So when I opened my eyes again
I prayed
And got up

Used

One day
I asked God to use me
Instead of allowing the devil to accuse me
Before I lose me
I asked God to use me
His response was
"Daughter
I will do just that
I will take your brokenness
And put some cream on it for it to heal
But before you ask for restoration
I need you to be still
Learn how to heal even in the midst of your pain
Take all the doubt in your mind
Cast it down the drain
Heal daughter
Turn your words so they will be positively spoken
Learn how to minister
Even though you feel broken"
I asked to be used
He answered my call
Although He said He would never leave me
Nor forsake me
My presence needed to be present in the midst of it all
"Are you willing"
Is what He asked
"Are you faithful

Are you sure
Because in order to be used
To be elevated
Will you endure
Or ignore
Because you cannot minister or overcome
If you are stubborn like kids
How dare you ask for a blessing
When you won't acknowledge what the problem is
Are you faithful daughter
You want me to grow your ministry
But instead of looking for a blessing
I need to know if you will suffer for me"
I said I wanted to be used
But I mean goodness
Does it take all that
"Daughter you are mistaken
Put your power in tact
You cannot be elevated
If you don't have faith in me
You cannot be used like Esther
With a Gomer mentality
To be used means to be utilized
To occupy
To resort to
So what makes you think I will present a promotion
Without testing you
I will probe you

I will Job you
To see where I stand
Be faithful over a few
To make it to your Canaan land
If I am using you
It is because you are separate and apart
If you feel sifted
Keep your faith in your heart
You want to be used
But let me just ask
Can you stand solid
Because you cannot have a mind like Judas
With the heart of Isaac
When you are elevated
When you are raised
You will have naysayers
Because they are mad that you are saved
They will persecute you because you smile
Toil with you to destroy
Be upset with you because you have peace
Talk about you because you have joy
Do you want to be used
Are you really sure
Because you will have to choose
To endure or ignore
You will have your face to the floor
Sending prayers up for sure
Being used means you may have to suffer

Or be tested

But know that you are worth fighting for

So do you really want to be used

Do you really believe

Be ready to be elevated

Ask and you shall receive

"Let It Go"

Jesus replied, "No one who puts a hand to the plow and looks back is fit for service in the kingdom of God." -Luke 9:62 (NIV)

This book is called "I Almost Held On" for a reason. I've always been a person who did not know how to let go. It wasn't only things that I would hold on to, it was people as well. My mom, Aunt Porcia, and grand mom used to always say, "Chenae, he/she is not your friend." I would get upset, defensive and tell them they were wrong. I did not realize then that they were only trying to protect me emotionally.

I'm a person who loves to see the good in people. I have a pure heart and a love for everyone even if I don't necessarily want to deal with you on a regular basis. This may sound cliché, but I try to exemplify the love of God on a daily basis. Having a pure heart had become a blessing, but it had also become a curse because I wasn't able to tell the difference between a great friend and a person who just took up space. My problem was that I put my emotions into everything. From that, I had to learn the hard way that letting go meant letting go completely but that was something I had to learn over time.

People think that letting go is something that happens overnight. But it is the total opposite. Letting go is something you work at. It takes time and energy to decipher what is important to you and how to get rid of the things that are internally killing you. Letting go is a process. In the process, remind yourself that if you grow weary, you will reap a harvest if you faint not. I always admired my cousin, Joshea, because I never really witnessed anything affect him. I know things affect him because he's a human being, but he always knew how to bounce back almost instantly in spite of how he felt. I always wanted to do that. Recently, I decided to take time to learn. I didn't want to hold on anymore because holding on meant that I was only holding myself back. God demanded that I be brutally honest in spite of what anyone had to say. You know what the bible says, "Obedience is better than sacrifice." For me, obedience was my only option.

Don't hold on anymore. Whatever it takes, be willing to hold God's hand and take the journey to freedom.

My Season #1

I stopped living my life for other people
At their approval
So I started a removal
A process of taking a life out of mine
Lives that block my sunshine
I was done
Listening
Feeding
And fighting for people who could care less
People who only brought me stress
I finally see
What the devil was trying to do to me
To be held in captivity
I was a prisoner
Wanting to be set free
So I decided to expose myself
Telling my support system my darkest secrets that kept me in bondage
After it came off my tongue
I realized that I was held hostage
To my own self
To my own friends
And even to my own family members
People who wanted me to be like them
Wanting me to do the things they did
And since I was a kid
I did

Things that made me be accepted
Not realizing that my life was hectic
My friends had strongholds on me that I didn't know existed
It perverted my mind and left me twisted
I let people speak death into me and I started to believe them
I focused on the negative things that felt like treason
And every reason I gave was because I wanted to be accepted
Not liking the fact that I was affected
By what people thought about me
So part of me was happy and part of me lived in misery
Until I told my truth
Until it set me free
Until I was able to share how I really felt
Until I started to actually love me
I decided to let go of people
Who didn't accept my decisions
Through that process I realized that my friendships was a cycle of repetition
I held on to people who God told me to release
It wasn't until I listened that I found the most peace
I'm not ashamed of my truth
I struggled mentally
But I got a hold on my thoughts
And I love me
No one can take away what God has built
Especially because I prayed for it for so long
The more growth I endure
The more I realize I was wrong

God didn't bring those people into my life for no reason
They taught me a valuable lesson
That not everyone deserves a place in your life
Because they will not always be a blessing

At The Forefront

I'm standing firm
Through every bit of strife
I'm on the forefront
In the fight of my life
No one can tell me
That I'm not under attack
Because my life has changed
So I'm not taking any slack
I am going to fight
I refuse to quit
Because it's not who I am
Nor is it in my spirit
It has been prophesied to me
That it would come
But I have been reminded everyday
That I have already won
So it doesn't matter
What I'm being attacked with right now and here
What matters is I am willing to endure
I'm getting rid of my fears
I have no room to be afraid
But even if I am I have discovered
That no matter how scared I get
I am already covered
God has given me confirmation
That I'm not alone
So when He speaks to me

I know I am home
I know I am safe
I know I can get through
Because this is only a test
God told me, "This doesn't define you"
Never think you can't endure a temporary season
You can get through
And even when others give up
God will never give up on you

<u>Freedom</u>

I withheld information
Locked it away
In a box where I told it to stay
I hid it
Buried it under rocks and bricks and cracks
Put a padlock on it
So it would never come back
I was going to take it to my grave
Never to tell it
Because judgments would fly everywhere
I promised myself that I would never sell it
Not to the tooth fairy
Or at a ticket booth
I told myself
That I would never tell the truth
But I got to a point where hiding it didn't work anymore
Because it was eating me alive
I knew if I wanted to be free
It could not hide
I had to tell it
And let people go in the process
My truth was associated with people
Who brought me stress
So I had to tell my truth
Unlock my box
Spread it across the table
Strip away that padlock

I had to tell every inch of my story
But I've hurt people in the midst
God told me what to do
I had to release my fist
I had to endure some scary nights
Waking up afraid
All because I had some secrets
I was going to take to my grave
No one understood the suffering
Not even the people closest to me
They felt hurt
But I had to find my own victory
Now I'm dealing with the aftermath
Of relinquishing my information
It took a while to find some peace
Through my own meditation
I felt obligated
Not to say a word
Because I was going to be judged
That's what I heard
I felt obligated
To be someone's friend
I knew if I held on
It would never be the end
So it finally feels good
To relinquish part of me
I knew if I didn't let go
I would never be free

Galatians 1:10

"Am I now trying to win the approval of human beings, or of God?
Or am I trying to please people?
If I were still trying to please people
I would not be a servant of Christ"
Galatians 1:10
The harsh reality is
I can't argue with that scripture
It's real on its face
And those words
I should embrace
Because only He can take me to a place
Where I shouldn't only see my face
So I will place His face there
Because sometimes I'm too blind to reality
It's me
I can admit it
It's in my spirit
I'm not perfect
I confess
But I can address
The issues
Or the questions I have for everyone
Like why is it that when the sun comes up
And the light is on
I can feel you near
But when it's dark outside

I feel your rear
Sometimes I think
"Ok I'm going to take a break from the public
No facebook, no instagram, no twitter, no say
Just so I can see who is going to pick up to phone to call me
And ask me about my day"
Then I remember
"Oh yes
I'm the one who does the checking
I'm the one who does the phone calls, the voicemails, and good morning texting"
Talking other people off ledges
When sometimes I need to be talked off of my own
So it takes less than five minutes to check on someone
Come out of yourself for a second
And pick up your phone
Someone told me one day
"Focus on the positive"
I should
That's true
But people forget that silence can be violent too
And as I make my discussion
I realize
We may be adults
But sometimes
We have the minds of kids
So I have to ask myself
Am I trying to seek the approval of people

Or am I seeking His
Change your perspective
Because life should be smiles and fervent
I've learned the hard way that if you are trying to seek the approval of people
It's almost impossible to be His servant

I Am Willing

I am willing

Above all the fleshly desires of my own heart

Arrest me with the desires that you wanted me to have from the start

God

I am willing

To take on everything you place in front of me

Just to bring me through

Exemplifying your mercy and your glory

Willing

Yes God

I am

Show me more than a few

I am willing to forsake all others

Just to be with You

The One who created this heart

And had it under abduction

The One who never left me

When this person was under construction

Take me God

Hold me in your being

Guide me through my process

When my eyes are not seeing

When my body is anxious

When my mind is confused

Bring me to your bosom

And remind me that I'm being used

God
Remind me
Hide me
Guide me
Thank you for finding me
For minding me
For being kind to me
For blinding me
Yes God
I am willing
Arrest me in your spirit
Create in me something new
Something so powerful
That I cannot fear it
I am willing
God
I am
Take me through
It is a privilege
An honor
To be used by You

Elephant

I tried fitting in
In every way
From the day I got here
I tried being part of the crew
Until my face turned blue
I tried
I
Put on a smile like I was one of them
A person who wanted to have all the friends
And wins
Instead of losses
I tried putting on all black
So my flesh would blend in with theirs
Manipulating my own personality
As if my losses weren't wins
I have the greatest pigmentation in my skin
Telling me that I have the ability to be free
Me
A person whose ancestors fought for 300 years to show who they are
I am a star
One who is an ex-doubter
Ex-teaser
Ex-mind reader
And most importantly
I am an ex-people pleaser
Here I am

Being born again
Into a better friend than I was before
Showing the inner me instead of trying to fit into an already closed door
I am my own crew
Brewing the very foundation of my future family
Telling my unborn children that they should let their spirit and the Holy Spirit to cuddle
That there is a difference from an attack and a struggle
That when sin is pinned against you
Don't conform
Get into a huddle
And tell that muddled creature
That your spirit is not subtle enough to give in
It's not delicate enough to be naïve and give into the weed
Made out of trees that people have tried to blow into your spirit
It shows its endurance
You can't manipulate it enough like a progressive commercial to buy its insurance
Your spirit has its own
It grows into the very being that fits your tone
It shapes you into the person who has grown
That God has built up in order to call home
It's not about what others say about your situation
No matter the advice you get
Nothing can compare or trump
What God has placed in your spirit
But to hear it

You have to block every voice
Out of your spirit
Tell yourself that you are not perfect
But you are worth so much more
And no matter who leaves you
Keep in mind that you are worth fighting for
Stand firm in what He tells you
Seeking advice is an attraction
But the only thing I have learned
Is that it can be a distraction
A reaction you didn't want
Sentiments you didn't ask for
Even though you aren't perfect
You are worth so much more
You are not a mistake
And even though you aren't perfect
God adores you
You are absolutely worth it
And if you don't fit in
You're not supposed to
Because the person should be comfortable
With just being you
No attraction to crowds
Bury that in a tomb
And be comfortable with standing out
Like the biggest elephant in the room
Make decisions for you
Stand out and be different

Make a declaration to yourself
That you are tired of being consistently inconsistent
Declare that people will not be your downfall
Dust yourself off and keep walking in a different way
Because no matter what has happened in your reality
God still has the final say

<u>Blessed</u>

Smile for me
And I'll smile back
And as I work
Work with me
See the happiness written across my face
I pace in my space
Pace smoothly
Surely I have won
The sun has shined over me
So gracefully
Living here so peacefully
Even if chaos surrounds me
I smile
No longer stressed
I smile
Because I'm blessed

I'm A Follower

Living with uncertainty can be one of the hardest things to do
Especially when the focus is always on you
The spotlight is head on
Your peace might be gone
But you can't show it
Uncertainty is hard to do
Especially when everyone is watching you
So God comes in to hold your hand
Helping you understand
What has left you or hurt you
Or healed you or delivered you
What will bring you to victory
The feeling of joy
Being set free
Gee
God I wish you were tangible
Sometimes it's hard when your person is not understandable
When the journey you have placed me on can be filled with uncertainty
And all I have to hold on to is what you have constantly told me
When the essence of life is not always relaxing
And no one wants to admit that being a Christian can be taxing
When you consistently have to claim that you are a winner
And you are too holy to admit that you are a sinner
Yes ma'am uncertainty can be tough
But the one thing I do know is Christ has been enough
He knows what we feel

From our head to the ground
He knows about the soul ties that need to be broken
The strongholds that need to be torn down
He witnesses our own
Even when we want to fold
He shows us the power we have
And the patience of Job
He shows us the Wisdom of Solomon
The obedience of Jeremiah
The prophet in Isaiah
The servant of Obadiah
Yes my God knows
He knows because He walked this earth
With 12 other men
Then He became us on the cross
So we can live as Him
He is three in one
The One who lives
I can stand in front of you
Because He forgives
And as He lives in me
Uncertainty is gone
He died as me
So I can follow Him home

"Moving Forward"

"The righteous keep moving forward and those with clean hands become stronger and stronger." -Job 17:9 (NLT)

Take your time, but move on…

One person who taught me how to move forward was my Aunt Porcia. She would hold me while I was crying, wipe my tears and say, "Ok niece, let's keep it moving." Moving forward is a choice. It's a hard choice, but it is still a choice. I say this because most of the time, we stay in the same positions mentally, physically, emotionally, and spiritually because we are not choosing to change or take a step forward. The more time you waste on staying where you are, the more time will pass you by.

Moving forward means "to make progress." Notice, it does not mean to be perfect. I make this distinction because people confuse moving forward with completely forgetting or being perfect. One day God told me, "Chenae, how can you forget the things you have encountered or the experiences you have had. After all, you cannot have a testimony if you forget."

I used to think that just because I cry or something pops into my head and I have a reaction to it meant that I had not moved on from it. Actually, that's not true. The enemy will always try to keep you where you used to be because the words "moving forward" don't fit into his vocabulary. Who are you to believe that the devil would not try to haunt you with the things you have already conquered? He is on his job for a reason and the more you try to move forward, the more he will try to get under your skin. The question is will you allow him to? I think not.

I can admit there were times when I didn't believe that God could push me forward. There were times when I would think to myself, "God can't bring me out of this." Whenever I would get into that mindset, I would go to scripture, watch a sermon, or do anything else to remind me that God is sovereign. I would say, "God, I believe but help me in my unbelief," Mark 9:24.

I was in the house one Sunday and I called my Aunt Ny. She reminded me of the scripture that says to put on the full armor of God and all that comes with it. (Ephesians 6:10-20). This is guarding your heart and your mind from the attack of the enemy simply because he doesn't want you to have a prosperous life by moving forward. God wants you to be your very best. Put on the full armor of God. This is the shield He has designed for you to move forward. Your breakthrough is waiting. Let's walk together.

I'm Next

There was a time when I was afraid

Of being made into the person that God wanted me to be

To be free in the gift of my creativity

There was a time

When I did not want to revisit my past

Because I thought it would last

And take me to places I didn't want to go

So

I didn't

I did it my way

Everyday

I did it my way

I got caught up in things that was none of my business

And allowed the devil to have a place in my life

I didn't take care of it then

I did it my way

And believed him when he told me that I would never be anyone's wife

Because what I did in my life

Was tainted

Red painted

I fainted then

And became acquainted when I was tainted

Instead of resting in Him

It caught up to me

Shame and guilt crept up

Until everyone was gone

And there was nothing in my cup
There was a time when I was so scared
That it paralyzed me
I tried to fix it myself
Instead of letting God sterilize me
When I cried myself to sleep
Because it was so hard to bear
When I woke up in the middle of the night
God was there
And there were many times
When I felt like I was by myself
And I said that I would rather die
Than to feel what I felt
That scared feeling of not knowing who you are
That hits your soul
When you are so used to being the navigator
But then you have no control
My plans fell apart
And voices started in my head
And spiritual warfare crept up on me
And I believed what they said
When people thought I was crazy
I got myself into a rut
When I should have listened to God before
But I decided to empty my cup
I remember what it felt like
To lay in my bed
As I closed my eyes

And tried to shake those voices out in my head
When my niceness became my weakness
Because I felt like I loss
God stepped in
And gave me chance number two
When He reminded me of the cross
He told me to stay in it
When my low place was confusing
He forgave me
And saved me
When I didn't have the solution
When my mind went one way
And my heart went another
He told me to stay where I am
And not to go any further
So I stood in my mess
When I thought life was unfair
I didn't have anywhere else to go
So I stood even when I was scared
When I questioned who I was
Because of the pain I was in
God grabbed me
And held me
And told me I would still win
So who am I
Not to stand even when I'm afraid
No matter who I was
I now have the sense that God gave

So even though I was left
Because I was misunderstood
God told me to be free
Even when I didn't think I could
Restoration doesn't come in the confession
Or the gifts placed inside of me
It comes when you are willing
To go through the recovery
So when I was afraid I was influenced
I was scared all the time
I didn't know until now
That my transparency
And my willingness
Has me next in line

Here I Am

Here I am
Coming out of misery
I have rose to the occasion
While standing on the necks of my enemies
I
The person who was needy
Who held people to a high esteem
Who realized that I would make others happy
Before I followed my dreams
But here I am
Pleasing God first
Because He took me and dusted me off
When He saw me at my worst
Everybody was around me
When things were going good
Then I couldn't find a soul
When I was misunderstood
But who am I to be angry
Bitter or upset
It's ok because even when I was at my worst
God saw me at my best
When I was ridiculed because of my season
When my heart was broken and all I could do was cry
He wiped every tear from my face
Gently drying my eyes
Even when I tried to smile
I didn't know my purpose for a while

I didn't know my smile was worthwhile
Even when it is hard to smile
I have to
I need to
Because it wasn't like I was under a curse
I had to constantly remind myself
That it could have been worse
I attached myself to people so much
That I forgot about Him
A good friend told me
"You'd rather carry around dead people
Than to be without them"
That rude awakening opened my eyes
It hit me in a sensitive spot
Because you never know that God is all you need
Until He is all you've got
It took me a while to understand that I don't need people
Because I have the ability to be ok with just God and me
I had to get to a point where having people was a privilege
And not a necessity
Who am I to be upset
That things didn't go my way
I'd rather be under God's protection
Instead of being out of His Will everyday
So here I am
Smiling even when I don't want to
What God has promised me
Will always remain true

He will always love me for who I am and who I'm growing to be
As much as the sun shines
He will never stop blessing me
Just because the ones I love changed their minds
I will not stop living
Even if I'm hurt
Because I have the words "more than a conqueror"
Written across my shirt
You can't take away what God built
Manifested inside of me
Here I am standing strong
On the necks of my enemies

The Wedding

When Jesus came into my life
He told that I was His wife
A bride forever
With Him
I am hot
Constantly telling me who I am
While the devil tells me who I am not
I am with Him
By Him I live
I move
I love
I improve
Every day I am forever His
His bride
With a beautiful flowing white dress
I impressed Him when I said "yes"
Yes God
I do
I do love you
In every aspect of the word
For everything you continue to bring me through
God I am yours
For every mountain I have overcome
For every tribulation I have conquered
For every trial I have come through
Defeating my monsters
I am overcoming

Stepping over every notion
God I am arriving
I am no longer a prisoner of my emotions
Because when I was
I stepped away from you slightly
I wasn't in your presence
Because I didn't like me
So when you came to rescue me
I kindly agreed
Forsaking all others
I wanted to be freed
The backlash I wouldn't mind taking
My perspective was different
I own my part
Because I wasn't totally innocent
But God didn't care about that
He spit in the sand and cleansed me
Even through my filth
He still saw fit to use me
Other people's opinions didn't matter
What mattered was my truth
God took my pain
And
I became Ruth
A follower
Willing
Forsaking all others
Chilling

What mattered was what was in me
All of me
Not just a whim
God had to separate me
Hide me in Him
He told me to let go
No one would understand
No explanations were necessary
Because it was all in His plan
Everything I thought I needed had to go
That included the people in it
I didn't know that your thoughts and who you are around
Can affect your spirit
So I took up my cross to follow Him
What I got for free He already paid
I followed His instructions
And it was the best decision I had ever made
God
I do
Every day I will have you as the man in my life
Because you changed my inner man
The day you asked me to be your wife
I do

I Am Eve

I want to tell you a little story

About honesty

I caressed it

Married it

Declared that it wouldn't be a travesty

I am the uncommon generation

The peculiar person who would endure

Before I took the easy road

The appointed generation would rather be honest

Than carry a false episode

I am Eve

Having the ability to make the earth quake

She was deceived by a snake

Who disguised himself as her friend

Her mistake carried us to this end

But my mother Eve was amazing

Because in spite of her wrong

God was still gazing

Eyeing His creation

Like a father so protective of his son

Even through Eve's mishaps

She still won

She stood in her mess

And God was her assurance

Even though we struggle today

She birthed the idea of endurance

And the reassurance of His mercy

Makes certain that in our lives
The devil does not play the joker
If I didn't struggle my praise would be on the outer courts
My worship would be mediocre
Instead of God turning His back
Before the earth could quake
Eve was blessed enough to give birth to the nation
In spite of her untimely mistake
Adam was her husband
But God was her judge
And even when Adam was upset
God did not budge
He brought them closer together
As they grew near
In spite of Eve's mistake
We are all still here
My mother
And your mothers
And my grandmothers
And your grandmothers
And me
And you
We all have to receive
And believe that our insides match Eve's
Filled with mistakes and insecurities
But abilities to bounce back
It is the woman who is honest about being imperfect
Who has the greatest impact

The most love
The most peace
The peculiar story
We are the ones who overcome
By the power of our testimony
Eve was amazing
I am her daughter I know
God was upset with her
But His love never let her go
I am Eve
And so are you
And you
And you
The more I concentrate on His Word
The more its facts are true
Sin entered the world
Yes
But it gave us an opportunity
To experience the intimacy of God
Gladly revealing His mercy
God didn't kill Eve immediately
He saved her
Rearranged her
And changed her befittingly
Eve was amazing because she was honest
She started the peculiar generation
And even though her slate wasn't clean
She still gave birth to a nation

Amazing

I am freaking amazing
From the crown of my head
To my left big toe
I know
That I am freaking amazing
Amazing like the dew after a midnight storm
Or the earth's rotation after it's been warm
I was born to be amazing
Like the moon that looks down on the stars
Or trying new things even if they are hard
I am freaking amazing
Like my natural hair before it is blown dry
Or even if I cried the night before
God said He would open doors
And I've had to humble myself to the floor
Because wanting more has meant that I've had to endure
The ability to stand
I am unafraid
I am not fazed
Even when I am at my lowest
I am still amazed
By me
By what I can do
Learning how to stand still
In spite of the hater in you
I am freaking amazing
I love

I laugh
I live
I smile
I suffer for the greatness of God
Because it is worth my while
Freaking amazing
Like the gel manicure on my hands
And the Shea Moisture in my hair
By my ability to grow
Knowing that God won't leave me there
Amazingly amazing
Even when I am hit
I have patience enough to know
That I am perfectly imperfect
That makes me amazing

Opportunity

I collect flowers on my way to work
The kind filled with songs and poetry
As they bloom
I smile
Bringing out the essence of me
An opportunity to soar
To laugh
To enjoy
An opportunity that no one can destroy
I saw a different side of my dream
And I took heed
Especially because dreams are not one sided
A different perspective is what I needed
You are giving
You are caring
And I thank you for every minute
Because I didn't only get an experience
But your spirit was in it
So as I collect my flowers on my to work
Of songs and poetry
I thank you from the bottom of my heart
As you took me under your wing to teach me

Even Jesus

Open your eyes around this room
Stick a broom up to the ceiling
Dust off and bleach the stains placed on you
God is about emotional healing
Take the pieces of your life
Scatter them around
Don't be afraid to separate them
All over the ground
Now go to each piece
To see where you went wrong
Then allow God to heal that part
And make your weakness a place that is strong
Once that is finished
Confusion will decrease
Anxiety will lessen
Because each piece will be a place of peace
So open your eyes around this room
Shed a tear if you need to
Because although you feel a pressing
Or an intimidation
God is truly rescuing you
Hold on tight
Grab those you love
God will bless you with those
He has sent from above
Stay right where God has you
What He is doing is so pure

Even though where you are is hard
You don't want to move to a blessing that is premature
Stay there because you are in the action or process
Of being made ready for use or consideration
This definition is the meaning
Of the word preparation
So that hard pressing feeling you have
Is meant because God will keep His promise
When this is over He will make a doubter a believer
Like His disciple Thomas
Let's be honest
Because Jesus is
He suffered greatly on His road
Just like we did
So what makes us think
That Jesus doesn't understand
What makes us think He doesn't know where we are
Just trust His plan
Especially because He is allowing it
Especially because He experienced worse
Look at Him
Seek Him
He will lift your hurt
So look around this room
And stand on your feet
Because this is your season of preparation
Not your season to retreat
This is not your season to give up

It is not your season to shrink
It is not your season conform
It is your season to think
Think about where you are
Remember those pieces scattered on the ground
Because when you least expect it
God is going to turn this around
Jesus had a process too
And as He walked He kept growing
No matter how much pain He was in
Remember even Jesus kept going

Letter To Jesus

Dear Jesus,

Thank you for your mercy

Thank you for your grace

Every day you put a smile on my face

Even when my feelings are hurt

And I'm looking kind of down

You are the one who always fixes my frown

I love you very much

You are my number one

I haven't made my point

So I'm not even done

My life would be nothing without you by my side

You are the king above world wide

You help me find my way when I'm lost

I'm grateful because you died for me on the cross

I go to church to rejoice in your name

You are the Almighty

You deserve the fame

When I have tears in my eyes

And I have nothing to say

When I pray to you

My fears go away

When you're ready

You will take me home

I will see you sitting on your throne

The King of kings

The ruler overall

A miracle worker
I can recall
Your house of heaven is not cluttered
You ate well when you and the disciples had the last supper
When you died
They put you in the tomb where you lay
Even though you rose again on Easter Sunday
Believe that you are being worshipped
We are your people
And trust that your Word stays in me in everyday
Yours truly
Chenae'

Remarks…

"And after you have suffered a little while, the God of all grace, who has called you to his eternal glory in Christ, will himself restore, confirm, strengthen, and establish you." 1 Peter 5:10

When God called me to write this book, He told me that my testimony was important and that I shouldn't be afraid to share it. It was difficult dealing with all of the baggage on the cover and back of this book as well as other topics I discussed. The hardest part has been making the conscious decision to let these things go including heartache, suffering, and disappointments.

This book was not easy to write. There were days when I didn't want to write because I wanted to sleep or cry. Some days, it was almost as if God placed his hand in mine so I could write. There were times when I was so overwhelmed with these things that it would feel like the struggle would never be over. Every struggle has its end. You just have to believe that it will end in order to continue moving forward with your life.

Before you close this book, please take a minute to pray with me: *Father God in the mighty name of Jesus, we just thank you for bringing us here for such a time as this. We boldly come before you confessing our sins. We know that anything we do that limits our ability to serve you must be struck down and cast out of our lives. The enemy does not want us to win but he has no authority over our lives. We pray that every person who has an encounter with you will be changed for the better. Some people may not understand the journey you have them on, but God you have not called us to understand. You have called us to be obedient. God help us to live for you and only you. Help us to seek you first. Help us to live by scripture instead of just quoting it. God if we are comfortable in our torment, help us to step out on faith so that warfare, depression, suicide, homosexuality, lies, doubt, fear, deceit, hate, hurt, anxiety, murder, rebellion, shame, guilt, rape, molestation, or anything else that keeps us from you will have to cease. God we are no longer prisoners to the very things that the devil has accused us of. So God we pray that you have your way in our lives; that you be there for us and guide our way like never before. God you are so awesome and worthy to be praised. It is in your son Jesus name we pray, Amen.*

God bless you.

www.ingramcontent.com/pod-product-compliance
Lightning Source LLC
Chambersburg PA
CBHW071200090426
42736CB00012B/2404